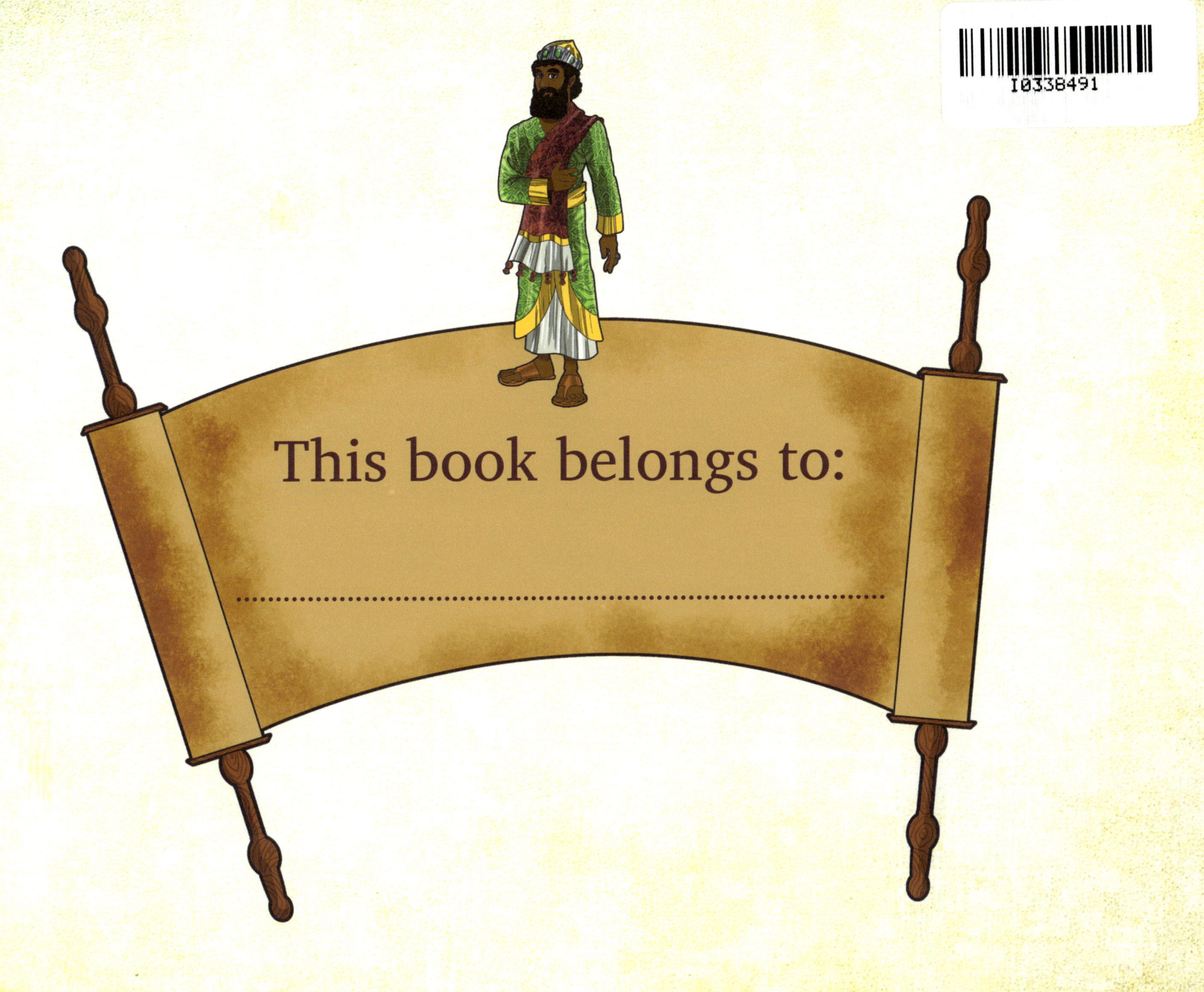

This book belongs to:

....

Copyright © BPA Publishing Ltd 2020

Author: Pip Reid
Illustrator: Thomas Barnett
Creative Director: Curtis Reid

www.biblepathwayadventures.com

Thank you for supporting Bible Pathway Adventures®. Our adventure series helps parents teach their children more about the Bible in a fun creative way. Designed for the whole family, Bible Pathway Adventures' mission is to help bring discipleship back into homes around the world. The search for truth is more fun than tradition!

The moral rights of author and illustrator have been asserted, this book is copyright.

ISBN: 978-0-473-40074-3

Thrown to The Lions

The adventures of Daniel

> *"My God sent his angel and shut the lions' mouths, and they have not harmed me, because I was found blameless before Him…" (Daniel 6:22)*

Young Daniel and his friends stared over the walls of Jerusalem at the fierce Babylonian army below. The prophet Jeremiah had warned the Hebrews that if they kept worshipping false gods, enemies would attack the city. Now the king of Babylon and his soldiers were here.

King Nebuchadnezzar and his army had come and set up camp outside Jerusalem. They were not letting anyone go in or out. The Hebrews ran out of food and their stomachs grumbled. They became so hungry that they threw open the city gates and let their enemies come inside.

The soldiers broke down the city walls and set fire to the palace. They destroyed people's houses and stole the precious gold and silver cups from the Temple. Then they captured many Hebrews, including Daniel and his friends, and took them back to the mighty city of Babylon.

Did you know?

The Babylonian army was punishment sent from God because the tribe of Judah was not following His ways. Jeremiah warned the Babylonian army would attack Jerusalem, but he was ignored.

Life was very different in Babylon for Daniel and his friends. The Babylonian people ate strange food and prayed to false gods. But Daniel and his friends stayed true to God's commands. "I will not pray to these gods," said Daniel. "They are useless. They are only made of wood and stone." Daniel's friends agreed. "We will only pray to Yah, the true God of Abraham, Isaac, and Jacob."

King Nebuchadnezzar liked the boys from Jerusalem even though they did not pray to his gods. "Daniel and his friends are smarter than our boys," the king told his officials. "Teach them about Babylon so that they can work for me."

The boys learned about Babylon for three years. God watched over them and gave them lots of wisdom. Soon they knew more than anyone else. When Daniel and his friends finished their studies, they stayed in Babylon and worked for the king."

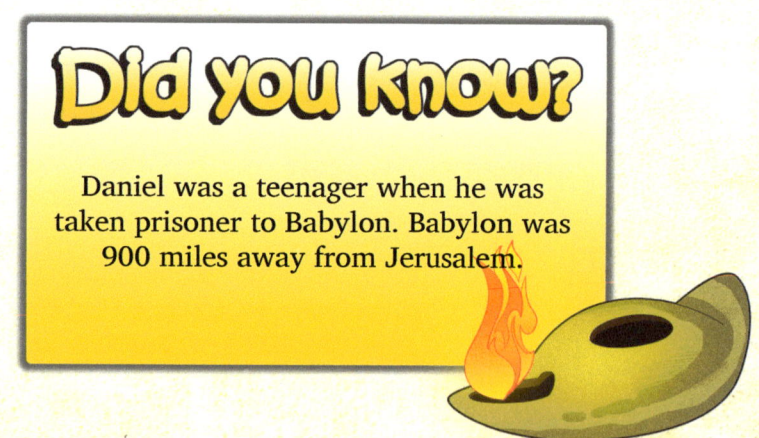

Did you know?

Daniel was a teenager when he was taken prisoner to Babylon. Babylon was 900 miles away from Jerusalem.

As Daniel grew older God gave him a special gift of understanding dreams and solving mysteries. But the Magi – the sorcerers, astrologers, and wise men of Babylon were jealous of Daniel's special gift. "It is our job to understand dreams and mysteries. How can this Hebrew know more than we do?" they said.

One night, King Nebuchadnezzar had a scary dream about a giant statue. His heart was filled with fear. He summoned the Magi. "Tell me the meaning of this dream, otherwise I will put you all to death." The Magi shook with worry. No matter how hard they prayed to their false gods, they could not explain the meaning of the king's dream.

King Nebuchadnezzar knew the Magi did not have the answer to his dream. He grew tired of listening to their lies. "The Magi don't know anything," he said. "Put them all to death!" Daniel, who had been sentenced to death with the other Magi, hurried to see the king. "Your Majesty, please give us more time. My God can tell me the meaning of your dream."

That night Daniel asked God to explain the king's dream. And God did so. When King Nebuchadnezzar learned the meaning of his dream, he knew Daniel was telling the truth. He gave him many gifts and made Daniel the chief of the Magi in Babylon.

Many years passed and a new king named Belshazzar began to rule Babylon. He didn't know about Daniel and his special gift of understanding dreams and solving mysteries.

Meanwhile, a king named Cyrus lived in a faraway land known as Persia. He had heard about the magnificent city of Babylon and wanted to conquer it for himself. He gathered all his soldiers, horses, and chariots, and set off to attack the city.

Soon, the Persian soldiers arrived at the city gates. Looking up at Babylon's enormous walls, the soldiers said, "How can we attack the city? The walls are as wide as houses. It looks like a fortress!"

King Cyrus thought for a minute and came up with a clever plan. "We don't need to break down the city walls. There is a river that flows through Babylon." He pointed to a huge pile of rocks near the river. "Use those rocks to block the river so the water will go down. When the water is low enough, we will creep along the river bed into the city."

King Belshazzar of Babylon was not scared of his enemies outside the city gates. "The city walls are high and wide, and our storehouses are full of food," he said. "There is no way the king of Persia can break down the walls and capture Babylon."

King Belshazzar threw a party at the palace to honor his gods. He invited the princes of Babylon to join him. The princes of Babylon liked feasting at the palace with the king. They put on their finest tunics and hurried to the party.

Trumpets blared and drums boomed. The princes sang and danced and had a party that lasted all night. Then King Belshazzar remembered the gold and silver cups his grandfather King Nebuchadnezzar stole from the Temple in Jerusalem a long time ago. His heart was filled with pride and he summoned his servants. "Bring the Temple cups so we can drink from them."

When the cups had been brought, King Belshazzar stood before the princes and filled the cups with wine until they overflowed. The people cheered and clapped their hands, and praised the Babylonian gods for their good fortune.

God was not happy with King Belshazzar's bad behavior. He did not want the gold and silver cups from His Temple used to mock Him. While the people were eating and singing, the fingers of a human hand suddenly appeared from nowhere and wrote four strange words on the wall near the king.

The king stopped drinking, the princes stopped singing, and the musicians stopped playing their instruments.

Snatching a lamp from the table, King Belshazzar strode over to the wall and peered at the strange words. His face grew pale and his knees began to knock with fear. "What does the writing say?" he shouted to his officials. "Fetch the Magi so they can tell me what these words mean."

Did you know?

Many people believe there are different ways to pronounce God's name. These include Yah, Yahweh, Yahuah, and many others.

The Magi hurried to the palace to see the strange words for themselves. The king said to them, "If you can read this writing and tell me what it means, I will give you many gifts." The Magi crowded together in front of the wall and tried to read the writing. But none was able to do so.

King Belshazzar grew paler and paler. "Why can't you useless servants tell me the meaning of these words?" he shouted. Hearing the noise the king was making, the queen hurried to see what had happened.

"Don't be scared," she told the king. "There is in our kingdom a Hebrew Magi named Daniel who can explain dreams and solve mysteries. His god gives him great wisdom. He will tell you what the words mean."

Quickly, King Belshazzar summoned Daniel to the palace. "Tell me what the writing says and I will give you many gifts and make you a ruler in my kingdom."

Daniel bowed before the king. "Your Majesty, I do not want your gifts. But I will tell you what the words mean." He looked carefully at the writing on the wall. "It says 'Mene, Mene, Tekel, Upharsin,' which means God is not pleased with how you live your life. He is about to give your kingdom to the king of Persia, and you will soon die."

That very night the Persian soldiers waded through the river, crept under the city walls, and invaded the city of Babylon. Hearing the Persian soldiers in the palace, the king scrambled under a table to hide. But the soldiers grabbed him and killed him, just as God had warned.

Did you know?

The message on the wall was written in a language called Aramaic.

The Persian army took over Babylon and a new king named Darius ruled the land. Babylon was big and powerful, so the king chose many satraps to help him rule the people. The satraps collected taxes and made sure everyone kept the laws of the kingdom.

King Darius heard that Daniel was the wisest of all the officials. He said to Daniel, "I will make you the most powerful man in Babylon, after myself. You can help me rule the satraps and the people." But the satraps were jealous of Daniel's special friendship with the king. "Why has the king made Daniel the boss of us?" they grumbled. "He is a Hebrew and worships a strange god."

No matter how hard they tried, the satraps could not find anything wrong with Daniel. He was honest and wise and worked harder than all of them. "We must do something to get Daniel into trouble," they whispered to each other.

Even though Daniel was the chief of the satraps, he didn't worship their false gods made of wood and stone. He loved the God of Abraham, Isaac, and Jacob. Every day, he opened the windows in his home and prayed to God. One day when the satraps saw Daniel praying, they had a nasty idea. "The only way we can get Daniel into trouble is if we get the king to make a law against Daniel's god," they said.

"With any luck Daniel will break the law," another satrap added. "Then King Darius will have to throw him to the lions." The satraps rushed to the palace and spoke to the king. "Your Majesty, we think you should make a law that says everyone must pray to you as their god for the next thirty days. If they pray to another god, then they will be thrown to the lions."

King Darius puffed up his chest. He liked the idea of people praying to him as a god. Before he could change his mind, the satraps quickly wrote down the law on a clay tablet and showed it to the king. "Your Majesty, sign here so the law cannot be changed." King Darius picked up the tablet, stamped it with his royal ring, and it became a new law in the kingdom. He had no idea that the satraps had planned a clever trap for his friend, Daniel.

When Daniel heard about the new law, he went back to his room and flung open the windows that faced his old home in Jerusalem. "I like the king, but I love God more," he said. Falling to his knees, he prayed to God, just as he had always done.

The satraps gathered outside Daniel's house and watched him pray. Then, rubbing their hands together, they raced back to the palace to tell the king what they had seen. "Your Majesty, do you remember you signed a law that for thirty days people could only pray to you?" King Darius' eyes lit up. "Yes, that is true; otherwise they must be thrown to the lions."

"Daniel didn't listen to you," said the satraps. They glanced at each other with evil grins. "He broke the law and prayed to his god. Remember you said that anyone who disobeys this law must be punished." The king clasped his head in his hands and moaned. "Daniel is my best servant. I don't want to see him tossed to the lions." The satraps crowded around the king. "This is the law of Babylon," they reminded him. "You cannot change it. No one can."

The king was determined to spare Daniel from the lion's den. He worked all day, but he could not find a way to save his faithful servant. "Why did I agree to be worshipped as a god," he said with a sigh. There was nothing he could do to save Daniel. With a heavy heart, he said to his guards, "Throw Daniel to the lions."

The guards quickly obeyed and led Daniel to the lion's den outside the palace. The lions hadn't eaten for weeks and their stomachs growled. Sharpening their claws on the stone walls, they looked at Daniel and licked their lips. Daniel's heart beat wildly. He stood at the entrance to the den and stared into the darkness. "I will trust You, my God," he prayed. The guards opened the door, grabbed Daniel by the arms and legs, and swung him back and forth. *"One…Two…Three…"* They tossed Daniel into the den.

Bump, bump, thump.

Daniel bounced down the stairs and disappeared into the darkness. King Darius poked his head through the entrance and called after Daniel, "Pray to your God whom you serve. He can save you." To make sure Daniel could not escape, the guards rolled a large stone over the opening to the den. Then the king sealed it with his special royal seal so no one could go in or out.

Inside the den, Daniel stood up and brushed the dirt from his tunic. He looked around. It was hard to tell where he was. Bats hung from the ceiling and water dripped down the walls.

Right in front of him, the lions strode around in circles, baring their sharp shiny teeth. They were starving and Daniel smelled delicious. Daniel stared worriedly at the lions. They were huge and scary, and looked very hungry.

But Daniel trusted God. He prayed, "Please save me from the lions if this is Your will." And that night, God answered Daniel's prayer. He sent an angel to shut the lion's mouths so they did not eat him. Instead, the lions fell fast asleep beside Daniel and snored all night. "God, thank You for Your protection," prayed a grateful Daniel. He knew his trust in God had been rewarded.

At the palace, King Darius tossed and turned in his bed all night. He couldn't stop thinking about Daniel in the lion's den. With all his heart he hoped that Daniel's god would save him.

Early the next morning, the king leapt out of bed and dashed to the den to see for himself if Daniel was still alive. He ordered the guards to break open the royal seal. Then, he poked his head through the door of the den. "Daniel, are you alive?" he shouted. "Did your God protect you from the lions?"

Daniel looked up at the king and answered, "My God sent an angel to shut the lions' mouths so they didn't eat me. He knew I had done nothing wrong." The king clapped his hands and danced for joy. "I'm so happy you are alive!" Quickly, the guards pulled Daniel out of the lion's den and stared at him in shock. They could not find even one scratch or cut on his body. "Daniel's god has saved him," they said.

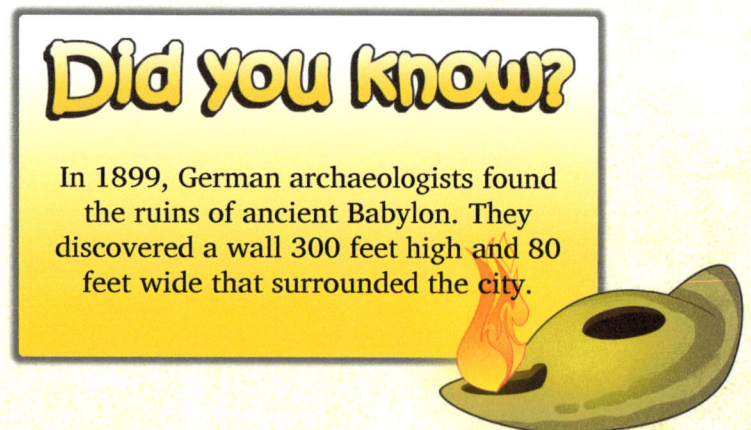

Did you know?

In 1899, German archaeologists found the ruins of ancient Babylon. They discovered a wall 300 feet high and 80 feet wide that surrounded the city.

Everyone was pleased that Daniel was alive. Everyone, that is, except the evil satraps. They were furious! Stamping their feet, they said, "Someone must have fed the lions so they weren't hungry. There is no way that Daniel's god protected him."

King Darius knew the satraps were wicked and punished them for getting Daniel into trouble. "Throw these men to the lions. Let's see if the lions are hungry now," he said. This time the lions were not so friendly and tore Daniels' enemies to pieces.

King Darius knew in his heart that it was the Hebrews' god who protected Daniel from the lions. He passed a new law that said all the people in Babylon should worship Yah, the God of Abraham, Isaac, and Jacob.

Then, he sent letters to everyone saying, "The God of the Hebrews is the only true God and He is the most powerful!" The king wanted the world to know that this mighty God had saved his faithful servant, Daniel. And from that day on, Daniel and his friends lived in peace in the kingdom of Babylon. They never forgot the night God saved Daniel from the lions.

THE END

TEST YOUR KNOWLEDGE!

(Match the question with the answer at the bottom of the page)

QUESTIONS

Which king laid siege to Jerusalem? ....

In Babylon, how many years did Daniel study? ....

What did Daniel do for King Nebuchadnezzar? ....

Which Persian king attacked Babylon? ....

Who threw a party at the palace for the princes of Babylon? ....

What did the writing on the wall say? ....

Daniel was put in charge of which officials? ....

What happened to Daniel after he prayed to God by his open window? ....

How was Daniel protected from the lions in the den? ....

What happened after Daniel was pulled out of the lion's den? ....

ANSWERS

1. King Nebuchadnezzar
2. Three years
3. Interpret his dreams
4. King Cyrus
5. King Belshazzar
6. Mene, Mene, Tekel, Upharsin
7. The satraps
8. Daniel was thrown into the lion's den
9. An angel shut the lion's mouths
10. The king ordered the satraps to be thrown to the lions

Complete the Word Search Puzzle

DANIEL MAGI
LIONS   ANGEL
TEMPLE DARIUS
BABYLON PRAY
KING   PALACE

```
D Z A J L D T H P B
B A P N Y D E B A A
A T R I G S M Y L B
V O L I G E P D A Y
P R A Y U Z L A C L
J T T H K S E N E O
L I O N S Z N I D N
R K G K I N G E J I
T V L V M N N L Y O
M A G I L I E U C I
```

Bible Pathway Adventures®

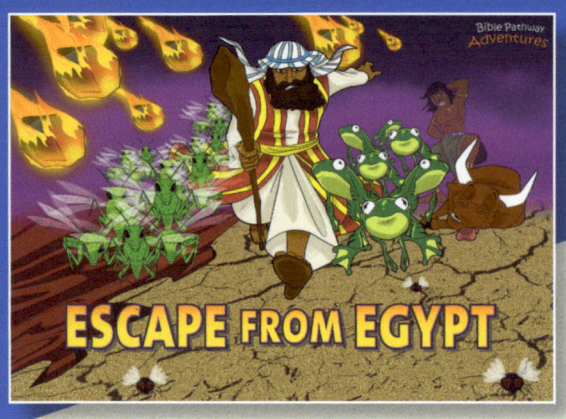
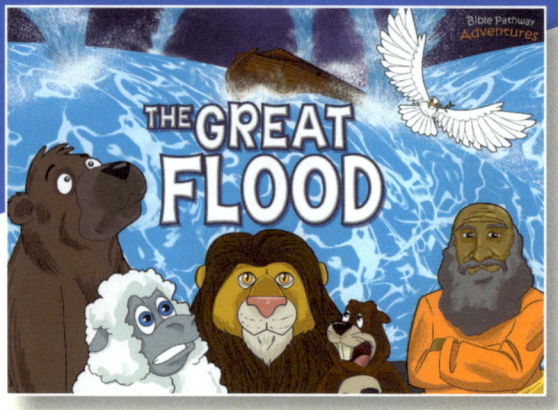
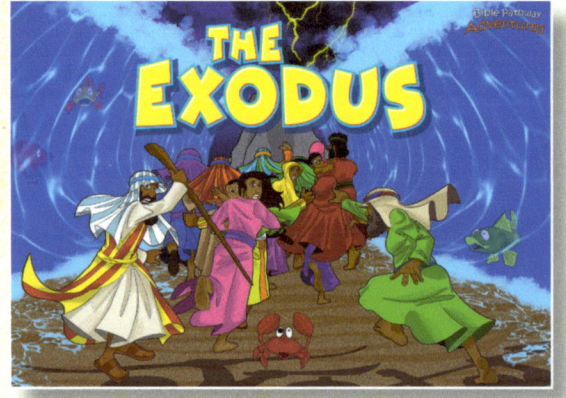

Swallowed by a Fish
Saved by a Donkey
Witch of Endor
Sold into Slavery
Shipwrecked!
Escape from Egypt
The Exodus
The Chosen Bride
Birth of the King
Betrayal of the King
The Risen King
Facing the Giant
Solomon

Discover more Bible Pathway Adventures' Bible stories!

Check out Bible Pathway Adventures' Activity Books

 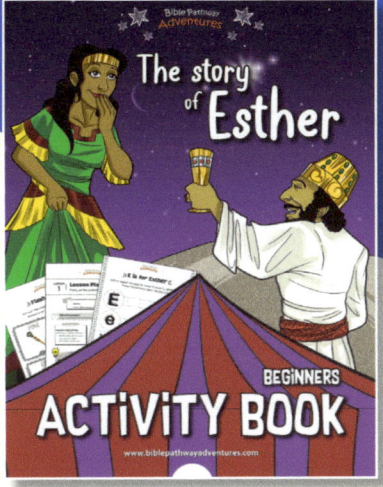 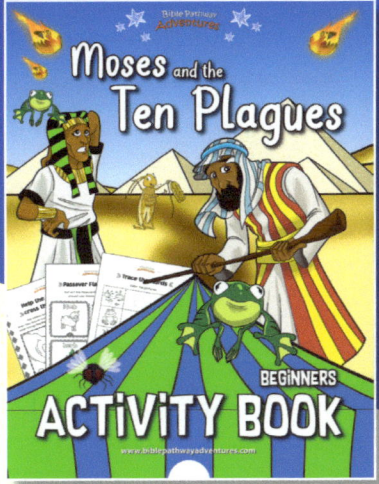 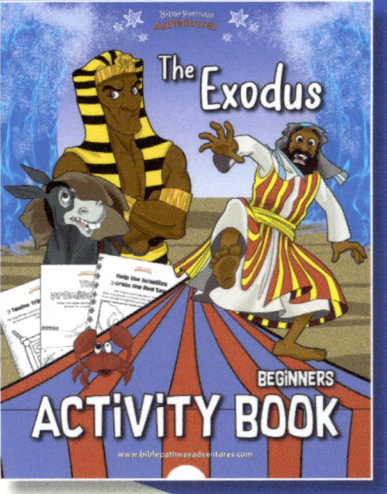

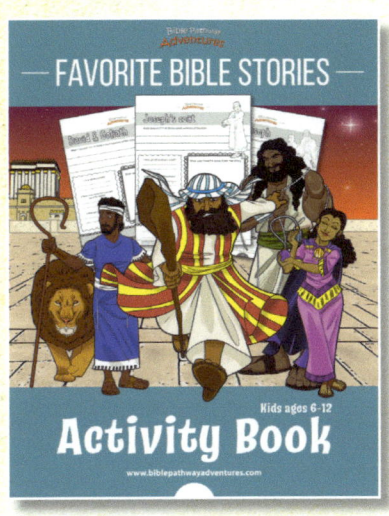  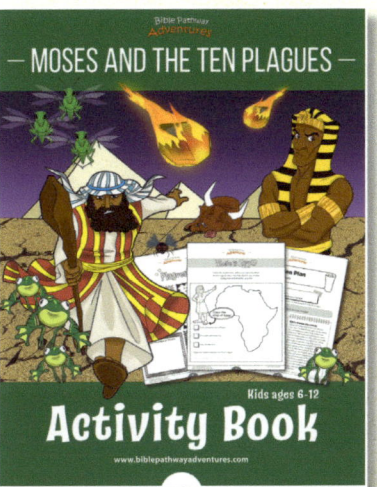 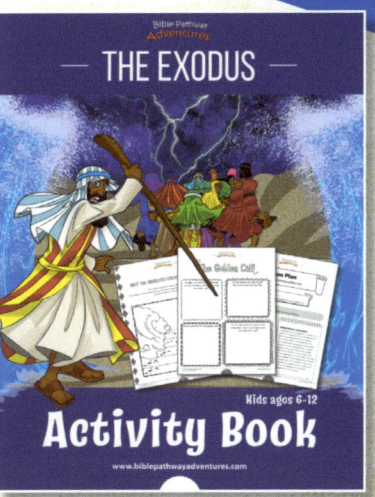

GO TO

www.biblepathwayadventures.com